Spiders

Words by Dean Morris

Raintree Childrens Books

Milwaukee

Cover Photo: Milwaukee Public Museum

Library of Congress Number: 87-16695

2 3 4 5 6 7 8 9 92 91 90 89 88

Printed and bound in the United States of America

Library of Congress Cataloging in Publication Data

Morris, Dean.
  Spiders.

  Bibliography: p. 47
  Summary: An introduction to various species of spiders, their physical characteristics, and their behavior patterns.
  1. Spiders—Juvenile literature. [1. Spiders]
I. Title.
QL458.4.M67 1987   595.4'4   86-16695
ISBN 0-8172-3213-3 (lib. bdg.)
ISBN 0-8172-3238-9 (softcover)

This book has been reviewed
for accuracy by

John M. Condit
Curator, Division of Reptiles and Amphibians
The Ohio State University Museum of Zoology

Spiders

There are thousands of different kinds of spiders in the world. Some are very big. Some are so small that you can hardly see them.

Many spiders trap their food in webs. But not all spiders make webs. Some dig homes under the ground. They come out to hunt their food. Some spiders hide in flowers. Others live in people's houses. There are even spiders that live underwater.

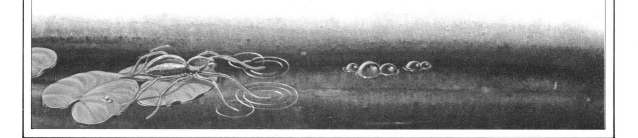

This is a garden spider. It has eight legs, like all spiders. Its body has two parts, with a waist in between.

All spiders make silk in glands inside their bodies. A spider has spinnerets at the end of its body for releasing the silk.

garden spider

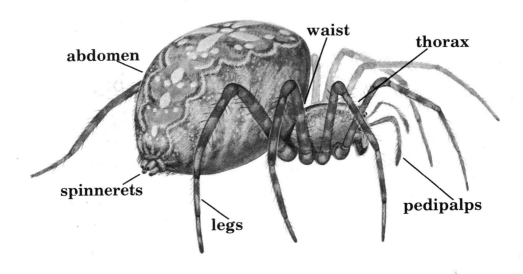

abdomen

waist

thorax

spinnerets

legs

pedipalps

spider's leg

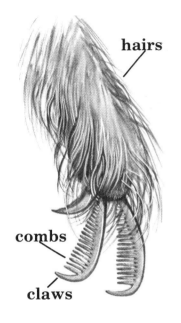

hairs

combs

claws

Some spiders have claws like small combs at the end of each leg. These are used to comb out the silk as it leaves the spinnerets.

Most spiders have more than two eyes. But they do not see very well. Most spiders "see" by feeling. They use their legs and pedipalps to feel.

spider's face

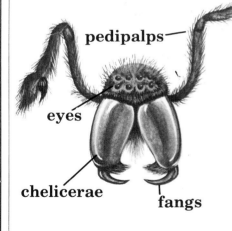

pedipalps

eyes

chelicerae

fangs

Spiders have big fangs. They use them to poison their prey. Large jaws, called chelicerae, help them carry and eat the food they hunt.

A garden spider starts its web with a line of silk. First it makes a silk frame.

Then it runs to the middle of the top line. It fastens a line of silk there and drops to the bottom.

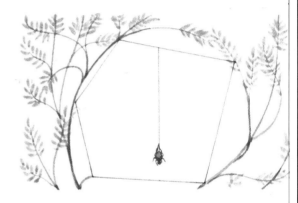

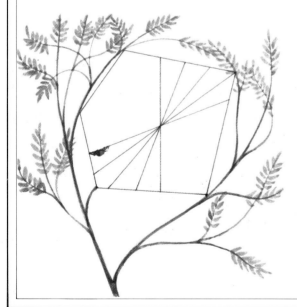

Then it moves halfway back. From this point in the middle the spider runs lines to all parts of the frame.

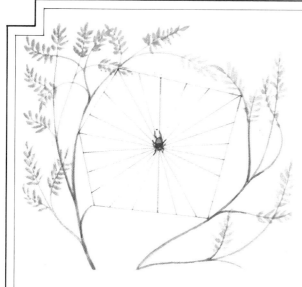

Now the web has a pattern. It looks like the spokes of a wheel. There are about thirty spokes. The spider moves around the center.

It fastens a line whenever it crosses a spoke. It makes wider and wider circles until the web is finished.

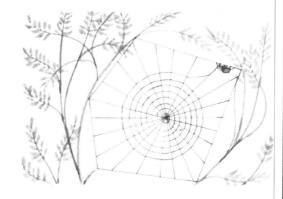

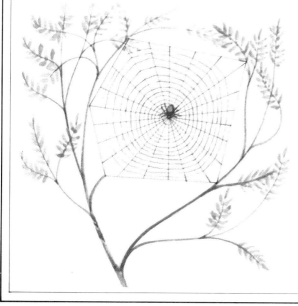

Then the spider lays down threads which catch insects. As the spider attaches these threads it gives a quick pull. Sticky beads form.

The spider leaves the
web to hide. As it goes,
it spins a line from the
middle of the web to the
hiding place. Then the
spider sits and waits.

An insect flies into the web.
The web shakes as the insect tries to get
free. The spider's line shakes too. The
spider comes running over. It wraps the
insect in silk. Then it paralyzes the
insect with its fangs.

If the spider is hungry, it eats the
insect on the spot. If not, it saves the
food for later.

Other spiders have different ways of making a web. This spider makes a "funnel" web. The top is big and the bottom is small. The web is held in place with lines of silk.

The spider sits at the bottom of the web and waits for an insect to trip over the lines that hold the web.

funnel web

This spider's web is shaped like a triangle. It is held to a tree at two points. The spider holds a line that is fastened to the third point. It waits. When an insect flies into the web, the spider lets its line hang loose. The insect gets caught in the net.

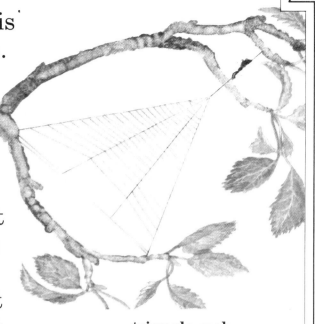

triangle web

lasso trap

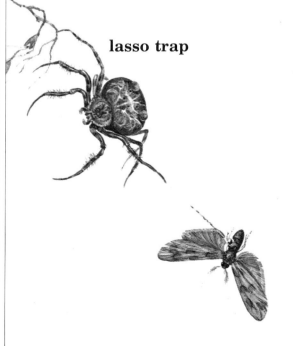

This spider works like a cowboy. It swings a line of silk like a lasso. At the end is a bit of glue. When an insect gets stuck in the glue, the spider pulls in the line.

house spider

This is one kind of house spider. It spins its web in dark places and in the corners of rooms. It makes webs in garages and sheds too.

This house spider's web is a tangled mass of silk. The spider sits in a dark corner of the web. When an insect is trapped, the spider runs out to get it. Then the spider fixes the hole in the web.

Here is another indoor spider. It makes a web that looks like big sheets of silk. It is called the cardinal spider. It is about twice as large as other house spiders.

The spider got its name from an important church leader. People say that long ago it ran across the floor of a palace in England. Cardinal Wolsey lived in the palace. He was frightened by the big spider. This spider has been called the cardinal spider ever since. This story shows how some animals get their common names.

cardinal spider

house spider

Hunting spiders do not spin webs. Some live under the ground in holes. They leave their holes to hunt insects. The female spider lays her eggs in a silk cocoon. She carries the cocoon around with her.

hunting spider

cocoon

When the eggs hatch, about 200 little spiders climb on their mother's back. They ride around there for about six weeks. Then they climb down.

Each young spider puts out a line of silk. The silk floats on the air like a balloon. It carries the spider to a new home.

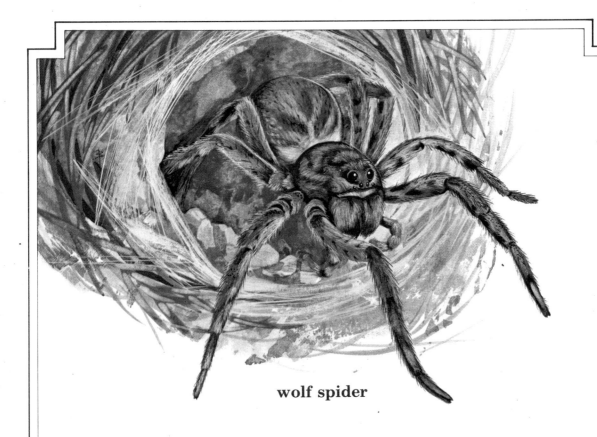

wolf spider

The wolf spider is another hunter. It lives in some parts of North America. It runs after insects and poisons them with its fangs.

The wolf spider looks dangerous, but its poison does not kill people.

The zebra spider is a jumping spider. Like a cat, it creeps up softly on its prey. When it gets close enough, it jumps on the insect.

Sometimes the male does a dance that attracts a female. She may respond by killing and eating the male.

zebra spiders

Crab spiders hide in flowers that are the same color as their bodies. They look as if they are part of the flower. Insects cannot see them. Crab spiders wait for insects to come to the flower. Then they catch their prey.

crab spider

Crab spiders can walk sideways and even backward, as crabs do. That is how the spider got its name.

crab spider

Some animals eat spiders. Not many animals eat ants because they taste bad. One kind of spider is protected because it looks like an ant. It is called an ant mimic.

ants

ant mimic spider

Trap-door spiders dig holes in the ground with their fangs. The hole is shaped like a tube. They line the inside with silk.

This trap-door spider makes a thick door for its home. The door is shaped like a bottle cork. It is made of silk and soil. When the spider is inside holding the door closed, it is very hard for enemies to open it from the outside.

trap-door spider

cork door

Another trap-door spider makes a different kind of door. The door is thin and has a hinge. It is not as strong as the cork door. Some animals can get this wafer door open. So the spider may make a second door underground to hide behind.

It may even dig places that branch out from its hole. When an enemy insect breaks in, the spider runs into one of the branches and closes the door. The spider is safe, and the enemy is trapped!

— wafer door

This trap-door spider never leaves home. It does not even build a door.

The top of its silk tube lies along the ground. The spider waits for an insect to walk over its tube. Then it runs up and grabs its prey through the wall.

The spider pulls the insect inside and paralyzes it. Then it fixes the hole and eats the insect.

Here you can see the spider inside its closed tube.

Tarantulas are the largest spiders. Some tarantulas are as large as a person's fist. Tarantulas can kill small animals, such as mice. Their poison is not strong enough to kill people.

tarantula

fisher spider

    This fisher spider can dive underwater. It carries its own air supply.

    First it traps an air bubble. It holds the bubble around its body and dives. When it has used up all the air, it goes back to the top of the water for more.

The fisher spider lives under the water. It makes a nest by spinning a thick web of silk. Then it fills the web with air bubbles. Water cannot get in, and the air cannot get out.

The fisher spider eats small insects and tadpoles.

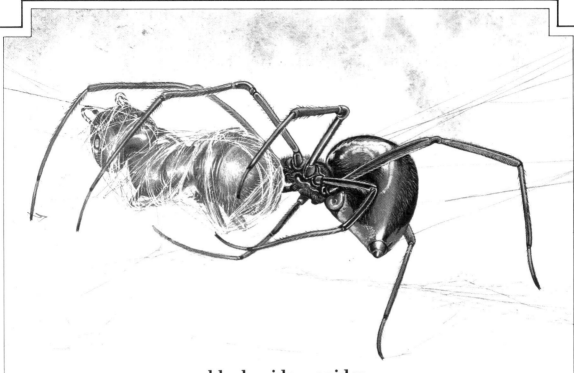

black widow spider

Spiders hardly ever bite people. If they do, their bite is usually not harmful. The black widow spider is one spider that is dangerous. Its poison may kill a person.

Spiders kill and eat many small animals, such as insects. But spiders have enemies too.

Spider wasps hunt and eat spiders. Ichneumon wasps lay their eggs on spiders. When the eggs hatch, the young wasps eat the spider.

Frogs and toads like to eat spiders. It takes a lot of spiders to fill up a toad's stomach.

wasp

ichneumon
wasp

toad

Scorpions usually live in dry places like the desert. They are fast runners. They have large pincers called pedipalps. The scorpion is a relative of the spider.

Some scorpions are dangerous. The scorpion has a long abdomen that bends over its body. At the end of the abdomen there is a poisonous barb. Some scorpions can kill a person with their poison.

scorpion

Daddy longlegs are also related to spiders. You can see how this animal got its name by looking at the picture. Most daddy longlegs live near water. They die if they have no water to drink. They eat insects, but they do not poison them as most spiders do.

daddy longlegs

mite

Tiny mites and ticks are both related to the spider. They are pests. Some spread diseases and hurt trees and crops. Others feed on animals.

Scientists call spiders arachnids. The name comes from a Greek story.

There was a woman named Arachne. She said her needlework was the best. She said it was better than the goddess Minerva's.

So the Greeks had a contest. Minerva and Arachne each made a wall hanging.

All the people came to see the hangings. Arachne's was beautiful, but Minerva's was even better.

Arachne felt so bad, she ran away and hanged herself. Minerva felt sorry for her. So she turned Arachne into a spider.

From then on, the story goes, Arachne made beautiful webs instead of wall hangings.

Where to Read About
the Spiders

Pronunciation Key for Glossary

a	a as in **cat**, **bad**
ā	a as in **able**, ai as in **train**, ay as in **play**
ä	a as in **father**, **car**
e	e as in **bend**, **yet**
ē	e as in **me**, ee as in **feel**, ea as in **beat**, ie as in **piece**, y as in **heavy**
i	i as in **in**, **pig**
ī	i as in **ice**, **time**, ie as in **tie**, y as in **my**
o	o as in **top**
ō	o as in **old**, oa as in **goat**, ow as in **slow**, oe as in **toe**
ô	o as in **cloth**, au as in **caught**, aw as in **paw**, a as in **all**
oo	oo as in **good**, u as in **put**
o͞o	oo as in **tool**, ue as in **blue**
oi	oi as in **oil**, oy as in **toy**
ou	ou as in **out**, ow as in **plow**
u	u as in **up**, **gun**, o as in **other**
ur	ur as in **fur**, er as in **person**, ir as in **bird**, or as in **work**
yo͞o	u as in **use**, ew as in **few**
ə	a as in **again**, e as in **broken**, i as in **pencil**, o as in **attention**, u as in **surprise**
ch	ch as in **such**
ng	ng as in **sing**
sh	sh as in **shell**, **wish**
th	th as in **three**, **bath**
th	th as in **that**, **together**

GLOSSARY

These words are defined the way they are used in this book.

abdomen (ab' də mən *or* ab dō' mən) part
of a person's or animal's body that holds
the stomach; the rear part of an insect's body

ant (ant) a small insect

arachnid (ə rak' nəd) an animal with no
backbone, eight legs, and a body that has
two parts

attach (ə tach') to fasten or join

attract (ə trakt') to pull something toward
itself; to appeal to someone or something

backward (bak' wərd) away from; to the rear

barb (bärb) a sharp, hooked point

bead (bēd) a small drop of liquid

body (bod' ē) the whole of an animal or
plant

bubble (bub' əl) an air-filled, round-
shaped thing made from liquid

cannot (kan' ot *or* ka not') is not able;
can not

center (sen′ tər) the middle point or part of anything

chelicera (ki lis′ ə rə) one of two fanglike parts of a spider's head
plural **chelicerae**

chelicerae see **chelicera**

circle (sur′ kəl) a curved line that is completely closed having every point on the line the same distance from the center

claw (klô) a sharp, curved nail on an animal's foot

cocoon (kə k$\overline{oo}$n′) a silky case spun by caterpillars and some spiders

comb (k$\overline{o}$m) a tool with plastic, metal, or wooden teeth, used to smooth hairs or threads

common (kom′ ən) usual, something that happens often

contest (kon′ test) a race or game in which each person tries to win

cork (kôrk) the outer bark of a type of oak tree often cut in a shape to be used as a bottle stopper

cowboy (kou′ boi′) a person who takes care of ranch animals

creep (krēp) to crawl or move slowly

crop (krop) plants that are grown for something useful such as food

cross (krôs) to move from one side to another

desert (dez′ ərt) a dry, hot place where few plants grow

disease (di zēz′) illness or sickness

dive (dīv) to go down through water headfirst

fang (fang) a long tooth, pointed at the end

fasten (fas′ ən) to put things together in a way that they cannot easily come apart

female (fē′ māl) of the sex that has babies or produces eggs

float (flōt) to rest on top of air or water or to move slowly through air or water

form (fôrm) to take shape

frame (frām) a support or border for an object

free (frē) able to move about at will

funnel (fun′ əl) a tube that is wide at one end and narrow at the other

garage (gə räzh′ *or* gə räj′) a building that holds a car or truck

gland (gland) a part inside the body used to make something the body needs or something the body gives off

glue (glo͞o) a sticky liquid used to fasten one thing to something else

goddess (god′ is) a female being that people think has special powers and can do things people cannot do

grab (grab) to get hold of something and quickly pull it away

Greek (grēk) having to do with the people of Greece, a country of Europe

halfway (haf′ wā′) midway between two places

harmful (härm′ fəl) able to cause harm or damage

hatch (hach) to come from inside an egg

hinge (hinj) a movable part that attaches

a door to a frame and lets it swing open
and closed

ichneumon wasp (ik ny$\overline{oo}'$ mən wosp) an
insect that is an enemy of spiders

indoor (in' dôr') inside a building or
a house

insect (in' sekt) a small animal without
a backbone, such as a fly or ant

jaw (jô) the top or bottom hard mouthpart
of a person or animal

lasso (las' $\overline{o}$ *or* la s$\overline{oo}'$) a long rope
with a loop, used to catch an animal

loose (l$\overline{oo}$s) able to move freely; not tight

male (m$\overline{a}$l) of the sex that can father
young

mass (mas) a large amount of something

mouse (mous) a small animal with a pointed
nose, a long tail, and a furry body
plural **mice**

mice see **mouse**

needlework (n$\overline{e}$d' əl wurk') work done by
hand using a needle and thread or wool
yarn

net (net) loose material made of threads or cords knotted together so that there are many holes, used to catch a fish, insect, or other animal

paralyze (par′ ə līz′) to make a part of a body unable to move

pattern (pat′ ərn) a way of putting together lines or colors or shapes to make a design

pedipalp (ped′ ə palp′) one of two feelers attached to the head of a spider

pest (pest) a troublesome thing

pincerlike (pin′ sər līk′) like a pair of claws that can hold onto something

poison (poi′ zən) something that causes a person or animal to get sick or die

poisonous (poi′ zə nəs) able to cause sickness or death by poison

prey (prā) an animal that another animal hunts for food

related (ri lā′ tid) belonging to the same group of living things

relative (rel′ ə tiv) someone or something that belongs to the same family as someone or something else

releasing (ri lēs′ ing) letting something or someone go free

respond (ri spond′) to do something in answer to an action

scientist (sī′ ən tist) someone who has studied a great deal about a branch of science

shed (shed) a small building used to keep things like wood or tools

sheet (shēt) a large piece of cloth

sideways (sīd′ wāz′) a movement to or from one side

silk (silk) soft, shiny threads made by some insects

soil (soil) the top level of the ground where plants grow

spider (spī′ dər) a small, wingless animal with four pairs of legs and a body divided into two parts that spins a web to trap insects for its food

spin (spin) to twist fibers together to make thread

spinneret (spin′ ər ət′) the part of a spider or caterpillar that produces threads of silk

spinning (spin′ ing) the process of making thin fibers into thread

spread (spred) to cause something to reach many more places

sticky (stik′ ē) causing something to be held fast or to be unable to move easily

stomach (stum′ ək) the part of a person's or animal's body where food goes after it is swallowed

stuck (stuk) caught in a way that makes a thing unable to get free

supply (sə plī′) enough of something that is needed

tadpole (tad′ pol′) the form of a frog or toad when it lives in the water and has not yet grown its legs

tangled (tang′ gəld) twisted together in a way that makes things hard to straighten out

thirty (thur′ tē) the number 30

thread (thred) a long, thin cord spun by a caterpillar to make a cocoon

thousand (thou′ zənd) the number 1,000

toad (tōd) a froglike animal that lives more on land than in water

triangle (trī′ ang′ gəl) something that has three sides that are all joined together to form angles

tube (to͞ob *or* tyo͞ob) a hollow piece of material, shaped like a pipe, that can hold or carry liquids

twice (twīs) two times

underground (un′ dər ground′) a place below the surface of the earth

underwater (un′ dər wô′ tər) below the surface of a body of water

wafer (wa′ fər) a thin piece of something shaped like a round cookie

waist (wāst) the part of an insect that is found between the two parts of its body

wasp (wosp) an insect that has a thin body and wings

web (web) a network of fine threads that a spider spins

whenever (hwen ev′ ər) at whatever time something happens

wrap (rap) to put a covering all around something

Bibliography

Dallinger, Jane. *Spiders*. Minneapolis:
    Lerner Publications, 1981.

Horton, Casey. *Insects*. New York:
    Gloucester Press, 1984.

Oda, Hidetomo. *Insects and Their Homes*.
    Milwaukee: Raintree Publishers, 1986.

Penny, Malcolm. *Discovering Spiders*.
    New York: Franklin Watts, 1986.

Petty, Kate. *Spiders*. New York: Franklin
    Watts, 1985.

Podendorf, Illa. *Spiders*. Chicago:
    Childrens Press, 1982.

Pope, Joyce. *Insects*. New York: Franklin
    Watts, 1984.

Selsam, Millicent E. and Hunt, Joyce.
    A First Look at Spiders. New York:
    Walker, 1983.